# Gluten-Free

## BREAKFAST

# What is Gluten?

Gluten is a protein that is found in wheat, rye, and barley. There are many reasons people avoid gluten. Some people are allergic to wheat itself while others may have a sensitivity to gluten and just feel better when they avoid it. The most serious is Celiac Disease, in which the body produces an autoimmune response after eating gluten. The only way to manage this condition is to follow a strict gluten-free diet.

# No More Bread? No Pasta?

At first, going gluten-free may appear to be rather limiting. Fortunately, there are many more delicious foods on the gluten-free list than on the forbidden list. There are also more and more products, from cereals to baking mixes to pastas, which are now being formulated in gluten-free versions. These days you'll find them not just in health food stores and online, but also on the shelves of most major supermarkets.

# Some Good News

Spotting hidden gluten in processed foods is a lot easier now thanks to the FDA's Food Allergy Labeling Law that went into effect in 2004. Since wheat is a common allergen, any product that contains wheat or is derived from it must say so on the label. That means formerly questionable ingredients, such as modified food starch or maltodextrin, must now show wheat as part of their name if they were made from it (for example, "wheat maltodextrin"). Be aware that this ONLY applies to foods produced in the US and Canada. Imports are a different matter.

# More Good News

Look at your dietary restrictions as an opportunity to try new foods. Add quinoa and chickpea flour to your cupboard. Use corn tortillas to make sandwiches or lasagna. You'll find easy recipes in this book that are so delicious you'll forget that they're gluten-free. Healthy eating may actually be easier without gluten, too. Adding more fresh produce to your meals, eating less processed food and avoiding refined flour are all steps to a better diet for anyone.

# Gluten-Free Flour Blends

While there are many products that are now readily available in the supermarkets, they can be rather expensive. We have provided a basic flour blend that can be prepared in bulk and kept on hand for use at any time. Please refer to this when preparing many of the recipes in this book.

## Gluten-Free All-Purpose Flour Blend

- **1 cup white rice flour**
- **1 cup sorghum flour**
- **1 cup tapioca flour**
- **1 cup cornstarch**
- **1 cup almond flour or coconut flour**

Combine all ingredients in large bowl. Whisk to make sure flours are evenly distributed. The recipe can be doubled or tripled. Store in airtight container in the refrigerator.

*Makes about 5 cups*

# Cheesy Quichettes

**12** slices bacon, crisp-cooked and chopped

**6** eggs, beaten

**1/4** cup whole milk

**1 1/2** cups thawed frozen shredded hash brown potatoes, squeezed dry

**1/4** cup chopped fresh parsley

**1/2** teaspoon salt

**1 1/2** cups (6 ounces) shredded Mexican cheese blend with jalapeño peppers

1. Preheat oven to 400°F. Spray 12 standard (2 1/2-inch) muffin cups with nonstick cooking spray.

2. Divide bacon evenly among prepared muffin cups. Beat eggs and milk in medium bowl. Add potatoes, parsley and salt; mix well. Spoon mixture evenly into muffin cups.

3. Bake 15 minutes or until knife inserted into centers comes out almost clean. Sprinkle evenly with cheese; let stand 3 minutes or until cheese is melted. (Egg mixture will continue to cook while standing.*) Gently run knife around edges and lift out with fork.

*Makes 12 quichettes*

*\*Standing also allows for easier removal of quichettes from pan.*

# Bacon & Egg Breakfast Strata

8 to 10 slices gluten-free white sandwich bread, cut into $1/2$-inch cubes

2 cups (8 ounces) shredded sharp Cheddar cheese

1 package (8 ounces) bacon, crisp-cooked and crumbled

6 eggs

2 cups reduced-fat (2%) milk

$1/2$ teaspoon salt

$1/2$ teaspoon black pepper

1. Preheat oven to 350°F. Spray 13X9-inch baking dish with nonstick cooking spray.

2. Arrange bread cubes in prepared baking dish. Top evenly with cheese and bacon.

3. Beat eggs in large bowl; gradually whisk in milk, salt and pepper. Pour evenly over bread cubes, pressing down lightly until evenly coated.

4. Bake 35 to 40 minutes or until golden brown and knife inserted into center comes out clean.

*Makes 8 servings*

# Green Pepper Sausage Grits

2 1/4 cups water, divided

1/2 cup quick-cooking grits

1/4 teaspoon salt, divided

6 ounces fully cooked turkey breakfast sausage links

2 teaspoons extra virgin olive oil

1 cup diced green bell pepper

1 cup grape tomatoes, quartered

2 cloves garlic, minced

1/4 cup finely chopped green onion (green and white parts)

1/8 teaspoon ground red pepper

2 tablespoons chopped fresh parsley

1. Bring 2 cups water to a boil in medium saucepan over high heat. Gradually stir in grits; reduce heat. Cover and simmer 6 minutes or until thickened, stirring occasionally. Stir in 1/8 teaspoon salt. Set aside.

2. Meanwhile, spray large skillet with nonstick cooking spray; heat over medium-high heat. Add sausage; cook until heated through, stirring to break up meat. Remove to plate.

3. Heat oil in same skillet over medium-high heat. Add bell pepper; cook and stir 3 minutes. Add tomatoes and garlic; cook and stir 3 minutes or until softened. Stir in remaining 1/4 cup water until well blended. Remove from heat.

4. Stir sausage and any accumulated juices, green onions, ground red pepper and remaining 1/8 teaspoon salt into skillet.

5. Divide grits among four serving plates. Top with sausage mixture and parsley.

*Makes 4 servings*

# Buckwheat Breakfast Bowl

3 to 4 cups reduced-fat (2%) milk*

2 tablespoons packed brown sugar

1/2 teaspoon vanilla

1/2 teaspoon ground cinnamon, divided

1 cup kasha**

2 teaspoons unsalted butter

2 apples, cored and finely chopped

2 tablespoons maple syrup

1/4 cup chopped walnuts

*For a creamier consistency, use more milk.*

**Kasha, or buckwheat groats, is buckwheat that has been pre-toasted. It's commonly found in the Kosher section of the supermarket.*

1. Combine milk, brown sugar, vanilla and 1/4 teaspoon cinnamon in large saucepan. Bring to a boil over medium heat. Stir in kasha; reduce heat to low. Cook and stir 8 to 10 minutes or until kasha is tender and liquid is absorbed.

2. Meanwhile, melt butter in large nonstick skillet over medium heat. Stir in remaining 1/4 teaspoon cinnamon. Add apples; cook and stir 4 to 5 minutes or until tender. Stir in maple syrup and walnuts; heat through.

3. Spoon kasha into six bowls. Top with apple mixture. Serve immediately.

*Makes 6 servings*

# Breakfast Quinoa

1 1/2 cups uncooked quinoa

3 cups water

3 tablespoons packed brown sugar

2 tablespoons maple syrup

1 1/2 teaspoons ground cinnamon

3/4 cup golden raisins (optional)

Raspberries and banana slices

## Slow Cooker Directions

1. Place quinoa in fine-mesh strainer; rinse well under cold running water. Transfer to slow cooker.

2. Stir in water, brown sugar, maple syrup and cinnamon. Cover; cook on LOW 5 hours or on HIGH 2 1/2 hours or until quinoa is tender and water is absorbed.

3. Add raisins, if desired, during last 10 to 15 minutes of cooking. Top quinoa with raspberries and bananas.

*Makes 6 servings*

Breakfast Quinoa

# Buttermilk Pancakes

2 cups Gluten-Free All-Purpose Flour Blend (page 5)*

1¹/₂ tablespoons sugar

1 teaspoon baking powder

1 teaspoon baking soda

¹/₂ teaspoon salt

2¹/₄ cups low-fat buttermilk

2 eggs

2 tablespoons butter, melted and cooled

Vegetable oil

Butter and/or maple syrup

*Or use any all-purpose gluten-free flour blend that does not contain xanthan gum.*

1. Combine flour blend, sugar, baking powder, baking soda and salt in large bowl. Whisk buttermilk, eggs and 2 tablespoons butter in medium bowl. Gradually whisk into flour mixture until smooth.

2. Heat oil on griddle or in large nonstick skillet over medium heat. Pour ¹/₄ cupfuls of batter 2 inches apart onto griddle. Cook 2 minutes or until lightly browned and edges begin to bubble. Turn over; cook 2 minutes or until lightly browned. Repeat with remaining batter. Serve with additional butter and/or maple syrup.

*Makes 16 pancakes (about 4 servings)*

Note: If you do not plan on serving the pancakes right away, keep them warm in a 200°F oven.

# Denver Brunch Bake

2 tablespoons butter, divided

$1/2$ cup diced onion

$1/2$ cup diced green bell pepper

$1/2$ cup diced red bell pepper

$1/2$ cup cubed ham

6 eggs

1 cup whole milk

$1/2$ teaspoon salt

$1/4$ teaspoon red pepper flakes

4 slices gluten-free white sandwich bread, cut into $1/2$-inch cubes

$3/4$ cup (3 ounces) shredded Cheddar cheese, divided

1. Grease 9-inch baking dish with 1 tablespoon butter.

2. Melt remaining 1 tablespoon butter in large skillet over medium heat. Add onion and bell peppers; cook and stir 3 minutes. Add ham; cook and stir 2 minutes.

3. Beat eggs, milk, salt and red pepper flakes in large bowl. Add bread cubes, ham mixture and $1/2$ cup cheese; mix well. Pour into prepared dish. Cover and refrigerate 8 hours or overnight.

4. Preheat oven to 350°F. Sprinkle casserole with remaining $1/4$ cup cheese.

5. Bake 45 minutes to 1 hour or until knife inserted into center comes out clean.

*Makes 4 servings*

# Buckwheat Pancakes

1 **cup buckwheat flour**

2 **tablespoons cornstarch**

2 **teaspoons baking powder**

$1/4$ **teaspoon salt**

$1/4$ **teaspoon ground cinnamon**

1 **cup whole milk**

1 **egg**

2 **tablespoons butter, melted, plus additional for cooking**

2 **tablespoons maple syrup, plus additional for serving**

$1/2$ **teaspoon vanilla**

1. Whisk buckwheat flour, cornstarch, baking powder, salt and cinnamon in medium bowl. Whisk milk, egg, 2 tablespoons butter, 2 tablespoons maple syrup and vanilla in small bowl. Gradually whisk into flour mixture just until combined. Let stand 5 minutes. (Batter will be thick and elastic.)

2. Brush additional butter on griddle or large nonstick skillet; heat over medium heat. Pour $1/4$ cupfuls of batter 2 inches apart onto griddle. Cook 2 minutes or until lightly browned and edges begin to bubble. Turn over; cook 2 minutes or until lightly browned. Serve with additional maple syrup.

*Makes 12 pancakes (about 4 servings)*

Variation: Add $1/2$ cup blueberries to the batter.

# Banana-Nut Buttermilk Waffles

$2^1/2$ cups **Gluten-Free All-Purpose Flour Blend (page 5)***

$^1/4$ cup sugar

2 teaspoons baking powder

2 teaspoons baking soda

1 teaspoon salt

2 eggs, separated

2 cups low-fat buttermilk

2 very ripe bananas, mashed (about 1 cup)

$^1/4$ cup ($^1/2$ stick) butter, melted

$1^1/2$ teaspoons vanilla

$^3/4$ cup chopped walnuts or pecans, toasted,** plus additional for garnish

Maple syrup and banana slices

*Or use any all-purpose gluten-free flour blend that does not contain xanthan gum.*

**To toast walnuts, spread in single layer in heavy-bottomed skillet. Cook over medium heat 1 to 2 minutes, stirring frequently, until nuts are lightly browned. Remove from skillet immediately. Cool before using.*

1. Spray waffle iron with nonstick cooking spray; preheat according to manufacturer's directions.

2. Combine flour blend, sugar, baking powder, baking soda and salt in large bowl; mix well. Beat egg yolks in medium bowl. Stir in buttermilk, mashed bananas, butter and vanilla until well blended. Stir into flour mixture just until moistened. Fold in $^3/4$ cup walnuts.

3. Beat egg whites in medium bowl with electric mixer at high speed until stiff peaks form. Fold egg whites into batter.

4. Pour $^3/4$ cup batter into waffle iron; cook about 5 minutes or until steam stops escaping from around edges and waffle is golden brown. Repeat with remaining batter. Serve with maple syrup and banana slices. Garnish with additional walnuts.

*Makes 4 servings*

# Blueberry-Orange French Toast Casserole

**10 slices gluten-free bread,
cut into 1-inch cubes**

**3 tablespoons butter, melted**

**1¹/₂ cups milk**

**3 eggs**

**¹/₂ cup sugar**

**1 tablespoon grated orange
peel**

**¹/₂ teaspoon vanilla**

**1¹/₂ cups fresh blueberries**

1. Grease 8- or 9-inch square baking dish.

2. Combine bread cubes and butter in large bowl; toss to coat.

3. Whisk milk, eggs, sugar, orange peel and vanilla in large bowl until well blended. Add bread and blueberries; toss to coat. Pour into prepared baking dish. Cover and refrigerate at least 8 hours or overnight.

4. Preheat oven to 325°F. Bake 1 hour or until bread is browned and center is almost set. Let stand 5 minutes before serving.

*Makes 6 servings*

# Chorizo and Cheddar Breakfast Casserole

8 ounces chorizo sausage, removed from casings or sliced smoked turkey sausage

1 cup diced onion

1 medium green bell pepper, chopped

1 jalapeño pepper,* chopped

6 eggs, lightly beaten

1 cup gluten-free biscuit baking mix

3/4 cup low-fat buttermilk

1/2 teaspoon salt

1/2 teaspoon black pepper

1 cup (4 ounces) shredded Cheddar cheese

Sour cream (optional)

Chopped tomato (optional)

Chopped fresh cilantro (optional)

*Jalapeño peppers can sting and irritate the skin, so wear rubber gloves when handling peppers and do not touch your eyes.*

1. Preheat oven to 350°F. Spray 8- or 9-inch square baking dish with nonstick cooking spray.

2. Heat large nonstick skillet over medium heat. Add chorizo; cook 4 minutes or until browned, stirring to break up meat. Drain fat.

3. Add onion, bell pepper and jalapeño to skillet; cook and stir 6 minutes or until crisp-tender. Spread mixture evenly in prepared baking dish.

4. Stir eggs, baking mix, buttermilk, salt and black pepper in medium bowl until well blended. Pour evenly over chorizo mixture.

5. Bake 45 to 50 minutes or until knife inserted into center comes out clean. Sprinkle evenly with cheese. Let stand 10 minutes or until cheese is melted. Serve with sour cream and tomato, if desired. Garnish with cilantro.

*Makes 6 to 8 servings*

# Raspberry & Cream Stuffed French Toast

6 **ounces low-fat cream cheese, softened**

3 **tablespoons powdered sugar, plus additional for garnish**

1 **teaspoon ground cinnamon**

1/4 **teaspoon ground nutmeg**

8 **slices gluten-free white sandwich bread**

1 1/2 **cups fresh raspberries, plus additional for garnish**

3 **eggs, lightly beaten**

2/3 **cup reduced-fat (2%) milk**

2 **tablespoons maple syrup**

1 **teaspoon vanilla**

**Fresh mint leaves (optional)**

1. Preheat oven to 350°F.

2. Combine cream cheese, 3 tablespoons powdered sugar, cinnamon and nutmeg in small bowl; mix well. Spread evenly onto one side of bread slices. Sprinkle with 1 1/2 cups raspberries; top with remaining bread slices, pressing down gently to flatten.

3. Whisk eggs, milk, maple syrup and vanilla in shallow dish. Dip sandwiches into egg mixture one at a time; let stand 5 minutes or until fully soaked. Shake off excess. Repeat with remaining sandwiches.

4. Spray large skillet with nonstick cooking spray; heat over medium heat. Add sandwiches in batches; cook 3 to 4 minutes per side or until golden brown. Place on baking sheet. Repeat with remaining sandwiches.

5. Bake 10 minutes or until bread is crisp and sandwiches are heated through. Slice sandwiches and sprinkle with additional powdered sugar, if desired. Garnish with additional raspberries and mint.

*Makes 4 servings*

# Banana Chocolate Chip Buttermilk Pancakes

2¹/₂ cups Gluten-Free
All-Purpose Flour Blend
(page 5)*

¹/₃ cup sugar

1¹/₂ teaspoons baking powder

1 teaspoon baking soda

¹/₂ teaspoon ground cinnamon

1¹/₂ cups low-fat buttermilk

3 eggs

1 teaspoon vanilla

1¹/₂ cups mashed bananas
(about 3 medium)

Vegetable oil

³/₄ cup milk chocolate chips,
plus additional for garnish

Butter and/or maple syrup

*Or use any all-purpose gluten-free flour
blend that does not contain xanthan gum.*

1. Combine flour blend, sugar, baking powder, baking soda and cinnamon in large bowl. Whisk buttermilk, eggs and vanilla in medium bowl. Gradually whisk into flour mixture until smooth. Fold in bananas.

2. Heat oil on griddle or in large nonstick skillet over medium heat. Pour ¹/₄ cupfuls of batter 2 inches apart onto griddle. Place about 10 chocolate chips on each pancake. Cook 2 to 3 minutes or until lightly browned and edges begin to bubble. Turn over; cook 2 minutes or until lightly browned. Repeat with remaining batter and chocolate chips. Serve with butter and/or maple syrup. Top with additional chocolate chips.

*Makes 24 pancakes
(about 6 to 8 servings)*

# Banana Split Breakfast Bowl

2¹/₂ **tablespoons sliced almonds**

2¹/₂ **tablespoons chopped walnuts**

3 **cups vanilla nonfat yogurt**

1¹/₃ **cups sliced strawberries (about 12 medium)**

2 **bananas, sliced**

¹/₂ **cup drained pineapple tidbits**

1. Spread almonds and walnuts in single layer in small heavy-bottomed skillet. Cook over medium heat 1 to 2 minutes, stirring frequently, until nuts are lightly browned. Remove from skillet immediately. Cool completely.

2. Spoon yogurt into serving bowl. Layer with strawberries, bananas and pineapple. Sprinkle with nuts. Serve immediately.

*Makes 4 servings*